D1192943

Careers in
ENGINEERING

A Career In Electrical Engineering

Careers in ENGINEERING

A Career In Electrical Engineering

Bonnie Szumski

ReferencePoint Press®

San Diego, CA

© 2019 ReferencePoint Press, Inc.
Printed in the United States

For more information, contact:
ReferencePoint Press, Inc.
PO Box 27779
San Diego, CA 92198
www.ReferencePointPress.com

ALL RIGHTS RESERVED.
No part of this work covered by the copyright hereon may be reproduced or used in any form or by any means—graphic, electronic, or mechanical, including photocopying, recording, taping, web distribution, or information storage retrieval systems—without the written permission of the publisher.

LIBRARY OF CONGRESS CATALOGING-IN-PUBLICATION DATA

Name: Szumski, Bonnie, 1958– author.
Title: A Career in Electrical Engineering/by Bonnie Szumski.
Description: San Diego, CA: ReferencePoint Press, Inc., 2019. | Series: Careers in Engineering |
    Includes bibliographical references and index. |
Audience: Grades 9 to 12. Identifiers: LCCN 2018006111 (print) | LCCN 2018008520 (ebook) |
    ISBN 9781682823507 (eBook) | ISBN 9781682823491 (hardback)
Subjects: LCSH: Electrical engineering—Vocational guidance—Juvenile literature.
Classification: LCC TK159 (ebook) | LCC TK159 .S987 2019 (print) | DDC 621.3023—dc23
LC record available at https://lccn.loc.gov/2018006111

CONTENTS

ELECTRICAL ENGINEER AT A GLANCE

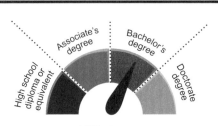

Minimum Educational Requirements
Bachelor's degree

High school diploma or equivalent · Associate's degree · Bachelor's degree · Doctorate degree

Certification and Licensing

Voluntary; although passing a Fundamentals of Engineering (FE) exam will qualify the engineer to work in specialties

Working Conditions

Indoors

Personal Qualities

- ☑ Detail oriented
- ☑ Mechanically inclined
- ☑ Likes science and technical subjects

Salary Range   About $59,240 ⟷ $146,820

324,600
Number of Jobs

Growth rate through 2026

7%

Future Job Outlook

Source: Bureau of Labor Statistics, *Occupational Outlook Handbook*. www.bls.gov.

A Profession for the Ages

It is hard to underestimate the role that electrical engineers have played in modern life. Nikola Tesla, an early electrical engineer who discovered alternating current and invented the Tesla coil, said over one hundred years ago that trial and error is at the heart of what engineers do. Engineers try to prove themselves wrong every day. Every idea, product, and invention is rigorously tested and retested to prove that it will work. Electrical engineers make sure that when a user comes in contact with an electrical device, it will perform safely and reliably.

Anything that requires electricity has been touched by the hands of an electrical engineer. An electrical engineer may work on any number of products, from small pocket devices that will allow a user to perform one task, such as connect to the Internet, to the largest of supercomputers that are responsible for driving the most complex weapon systems. Stop and think about the vast array of items used daily that involve electricity and it is easy to see the importance of electrical engineering in everyday life.

Adding Features for Users

As in any engineering career, electrical engineers start a project by setting the parameters of what they want their product or system to do. They use a computer to design the circuitry so that the product has the power and connectivity to drive it. A prototype is made and rigorously tested to see whether the product will work under the conditions for which it is designed. For example, a user may turn a cell phone on and off many times. The phone can perform this action daily, without having to be reset. Even when a device needs to be reset, it remembers the last settings it had and reverts to those. An electrical engineer made sure that the phone would be able to perform this and many other functions. Many products, including phones, continue to be rigorously tested for bugs. Many times, the phone automatically fixes these bugs without the user having to even think about it. Bug fixing is another part of an electrical engineer's responsibilities.

Many nonengineers have an image of the profession as being solitary, filled with geeky nerds who cannot communicate. However, an electrical engineer must have excellent written and speaking skills. He or she must not only communicate with fellow engineers—including engineers in other disciplines—but also with laypeople, including customers, investors, and company management teams. Communicating ideas in a coherent way that everyone can understand is only one part of the job. Every time an engineer changes a product, he or she must document it so that someone who picks the project up—sometimes even decades later—can understand the changes. The engineer must also pitch ideas and understand how to communicate them to others. Some engineers even claim that their English, speech, and humanities courses helped them as much as their math and engineering courses in getting a job.

As generalists with knowledge of many different sciences, electrical engineers can work in a variety of industries, ranging from pharmaceuticals to the military and even the arts and entertainment. This generalist feature of the career dates back to its very origins—to the days of Thomas Edison and Nikola Tesla. And although the world is much more complex than in their day, the field of electrical engineering persists and will continue into the future—as the people who build the electric cars that bear Nikola Tesla's name can affirm.

CHAPTER 1

What Does an Electrical Engineer Do?

Behind every electrical device is a history that includes design, testing, and debugging. Cell phones, microwave ovens, and computers all reveal the hard work of electrical engineers. Electrical engineers are engineers who specialize in the field of electricity, electromagnetism, and electronics. They need to understand these fields and how they work with power, control systems, and telecommunications. They also have to understand how to make devices communicate with one another and also within themselves.

Much of the work done by an electrical engineer is taken for granted by most people. Consumers might turn their phones on and off several times a day, but to be able to do that an electrical engineer had to figure out how much power is required to turn the phone on and off and how to conserve power when information is reloaded onto the phone. And that is just the beginning of how power systems work. An electrical engineer also designed the way in which the phone would deliver the power to its various components. And he or she would also have thought of all the ways consumers might use that power and how many applications they may have open at once. The engineer would have tested the phone over and over to seek the failure point of the phone and then debug it, or try to anticipate what the phone will do when that happens.

Many products today are designed using a computer. Because they work in a digital environment, electrical engineers usually know at least one programming language—and some know and use more than one. They use programming languages for writing code that controls the circuitry of a product.

Electrical engineers work on all sorts of technology. They might be involved in the design and development of communications satellites (pictured), household appliances, electrical power stations, or robotic systems—among many other examples.

Because humans are so dependent on electrical products, electrical engineers work on a wide range of technological devices. They design and redesign everything from household appliances to electrical power stations to wireless communications for orbiting satellites. Their work is not only diverse but also far-reaching. Essentially, a world without electrical engineers would be a world without technology.

Finding and Anticipating Failure

Testing electronic devices and systems for bugs is a major part of an electrical engineer's job. This debugging is especially important when an engineer is working on a device whose failure would have dire consequences. If one of these important devices does fail, the engineer needs to ensure that the device has a way of repairing itself or can be repaired remotely. For example, satellites are in outer space, yet technicians on Earth must communicate with them to make sure they are working properly. If something goes wrong, the satellite must be able to communicate what is happening and how it needs to be fixed. Another example is the complex circuitry within a fighter plane. While flying a plane, a pilot may receive a warning light indicating that something is malfunctioning in one of its systems. An electrical engineer designed the system that allows the plane to communicate the error; often, the engineer also designed the repair kit that allows the pilot to fix the problem on his or her own in the field. Changing out a circuit or running test equipment to help the pilot pinpoint the problem and fix it may save the pilot's life.

The work of an electrical engineer is also evident in the medical field. Electrical engineers are involved in the design and manufacture of microchips that run devices implanted in patients. Devices such as cardioverter defibrillators detect irregular heartbeats and deliver a shock to the heart to restore the regular heart rate. While designing a part of this microchip, the electrical engineer would have worked closely with other technicians, such as software engineers and computer programmers, who were also designing the device. In addition to design efforts, medical devices undergo many tests to ensure that they are reliable and will serve the patient for many years. The electrical engineer will also design how the device might be removed for reworking, fixing, and updating to ensure that continual bug fixing will be built into the device.

A Generalist with the Knowledge of Specifics

No matter what device or piece of equipment they may work on, electrical engineers begin a project by defining the product's function. They design the power supply, circuitry, and other electronic pieces needed to run it. Much of the time, an electrical engineer will have a store of knowledge that helps him or her know the basic parameters of every project. For instance, an engineer may be focused on an entire device or he or she may be designing a

Bringing Product from Concept to Fruition

Kathy Moseler runs her own small robotics company. Before she started her company, she had worked for Motorola, a large telecommunications manufacturer. In this interview, she talks about one of her proudest accomplishments while working for Motorola.

Inventing and creating are the best things about engineering. Creating something from nothing and then seeing it actually work is the best feeling!

There are two accomplishments I am most proud of. The first is being instrumental in moving technology from the Motorola Research Lab into an actual product. I did this for Motorola's first cellular phone that had videophone capability. I did not know it at the time, but it was my first job doing sales work. Success was driven by my passion for the technology. I have carried that through to my current sales work. The second accomplishment I am most proud of is that I influenced entire organizations within Motorola and companies outside of Motorola to work together to form an industry standard called OpenMax and then utilize it. It enables multimedia software to move more easily between different companies' hardware, reducing each company's software development costs. I did not realize it at the time, but this was my second job doing sales work.

Quoted in EngineerGirl, "I'm an Engineer: Kathy Moseler." www.engineergirl.org.

smaller component that must communicate with other parts of the device. Whatever the case, the electrical engineer must understand the larger project as a whole.

Once the design has been thoroughly examined and deemed workable, a prototype is made and tested. Yet the testing process rarely goes flawlessly. Debugging plays a big part of the daily life of an engineer. And this testing happens not just in the initial stages of a device or product. As long as the product is manufactured, the electrical engineer will be devising ways to fix bugs that might arise.

A Field with Many Subdisciplines

Because of the large number of businesses that involve electrical engineering, the field has many subdisciplines. Some engineers choose to specialize in just one subdiscipline, but others combine several subdisciplines to be effective in their chosen industry. A budding engineer may choose specialization while still in college or while on the job, depending on the needs and requirements of a particular company. Many of these subdisciplines overlap when it comes to work and responsibilities, but there are enough differences to deem them specialties. Examples include electronics engineers, signal processing engineers, and power engineers.

Electronics engineers specialize in electronic circuitry such as inductors, capacitors, and diodes. An inductor is used in electronic circuits to reduce or change the electronic current. A capacitor determines the electrical capacity of a circuit, and a diode conducts electrical current in one direction. Because of their expertise in circuitry, the electronics engineer designs electronic components, software, and other products. For example, an electronics engineer may research, develop, and test satellites, flight systems, and communication systems. Microelectronics engineers fall under this category also. They design and construct tiny electronic components, such as integrated circuits.

Signal processing engineers work with devices that produce signals, so they must understand how electronic signals are sent and received and how they communicate with other signals. An example of such a device is a fitness tracker that monitors the wearer's heart rate and blood pressure while exercising. A signal processing engineer would have designed how this device gathers the information from the body in the form of signals. These signals are then transmitted as digital sounds or a readout that appears on the device's display screen.

Power Engineers

Power engineers specialize in the design of electrical products such as transformers, motors, generators, and power electronics. These engineers are most likely to work in companies that deal with large power systems, such as boiler systems or electrical power stations, but they can also work in car engineering or nuclear power engineering. For example, the electric car manufacturer Tesla recently advertised a job opening for a power engineer. In the recruitment ad, Tesla emphasizes the importance of working with other engineers but also another role of the power engineer: managing a power grid, the system by which large generators bring electricity to the consumer. The job posting states:

> Electrical Engineering within the Power Electronics team requires and offers a very high level of collaboration with mechanical engineers and firmware engineers. Our systems typically deliver very high currents to enable our vehicles to go faster and charge faster than any other car ever developed in the mass market. Power electronics is the core of every [electronic vehicle]. Our systems control the flow of electrons from the wall to the battery and eventually to the motor.

The job posting also includes a list of responsibilities: "Design and development of power converters; Collaborate with mechanical, layout, and firmware engineering teams to successfully develop, test, validate and manufacture power converters; Start to finish ownership of hardware—from specification to design, prototype, and manufacturing."[1] From this ad, it is easy to see that although power engineers specialize in electrical storage and power flow, they must also be generalists who can work with the rest of the team on how such power will interact with the entire product.

"Electrical Engineering within the Power Electronics team requires and offers a very high level of collaboration with mechanical engineers and firmware engineers."[1]

—Job description, Tesla Corporation

"The Ilities"

Electrical engineer Rick Fulton works for BAE Systems, which produces components that are used in military applications, such as fighter planes. He says he spends the majority of his days debugging problems. He explains that one problem on a circuit board, such as debugging how the board communicates with other components in a system, may take days of effort to identify. Fulton says that the company uses the idea of "the ilities" as a way of looking at the work they do. When coming up with solutions, the engineer considers these questions:

- Producibility: Will the solution be simple to build?

- Reliability: Is the solution reliable?

- Maintainability: Will the solution be easy to fix and maintain? Will it be updatable?

- Testability: Does the solution have a built-in capability to prove the circuit works?

Rick Fulton, interview with the author, January 26, 2018.

Part of a Team of Engineers

Electrical engineers—no matter their specialty—must work closely with other engineers, such as mechanical, firmware, and software engineers. A single product design, for example, will involve the work of many different kinds of engineers. A good example of how the electrical engineer's role overlaps and integrates with other engineers can be found in the Brigham Young University's online course catalog. The site explains how various engineers contribute to the design of a robot:

> Robots are typically powered by electric motors powered by batteries. The design and analysis of those motors would likely be done by Electrical Engineers.

A robot needs the ability to sense its surroundings using cameras, RADAR, Laser rangefinding, etc. The design of those actual physical sensors would typically be done by Electrical Engineers.

At the heart of a robot is typically a full-fledged computing system which runs a specialized operating system and multiple applications programs. The design of that specialized computing system would likely be done by Computer Engineers. . . .

It is possible that the robot may need to wirelessly communicate with either other robots or with a base station. The design of the antenna for producing the radio waves used for this communication is done by Electrical Engineers. The development of the means of encoding those communications onto radio waves is also done by Electrical Engineers. The development of the silicon chips to transmit and receive that information is done by a combination of Electrical Engineers (for the analog circuits) and Computer Engineers (for the digital circuits and overall circuit organization). The programming of the communications protocols used is typically done by Computer Engineers.[2]

> "A robot needs the ability to sense its surroundings using cameras, RADAR, Laser rangefinding, etc. The design of those actual physical sensors would typically be done by Electrical Engineers."[2]
>
> —Brigham Young University course catalog

The electrical engineer is at the heart of many everyday products and other more complex systems, including the way electricity powers our homes, businesses, and public transportation systems. They must also assess the needs of end users and make sure the product fits the specifications of how it will be utilized. Finally, they develop systems to test and maintain these systems, making sure they run efficiently and can be repaired readily.

How Do You Become an Electrical Engineer?

Many electrical engineers recall having a penchant for math and science from a very young age. Others date the interest in math and science from high school. Aravinda Paranagama, an electrical engineering college student, discovered his interest in high school: "Ever since I was small, I liked taking things apart (not necessarily putting them back together afterward!). I was very curious to figure out everything, not just the electronic stuff. It was actually during high school that I definitively decided that I'd do Electrical Engineering."[3] Although it is not necessary to choose a career path as young as Paranagama did, an interest in math and science is a necessity for an electrical engineer. According to electrical engineer Craig Janus, if students

> "Ever since I was small, I liked taking things apart. . . . I was very curious to figure out everything, not just the electronic stuff. It was actually during high school that I definitively decided that I'd do Electrical Engineering."[3]
>
> —Aravinda Paranagama, an electrical engineering student

have the capacity to understand complex things such as math and physics, they might want to pursue something in the engineering field. Their interests will decide what area of engineering to get into. If they like to tinker, they'd make good electrical or mechanical engineers; if they like construction, they might make a good civil engineer; and if they can't get off the computer five minutes a day, they might want to get into computer engineering.[4]

Students must not only be interested in mathematics but also have a strong grasp of it; it is a critical component to learning and applying the principles of electrical engineering. WeUseMath .org, a website that describes careers that involve math, offers three main reasons why engineers need to understand math: "1. The laws of nature . . . are mathematical expressions. Mathematics is the language of physical science and engineering. 2. Mathematics is more than a tool for solving problems; mathematics courses can develop intellectual maturity. 3. . . . Computer programs contain mathematical relations; understanding these relations is still necessary."[5] Although electrical engineers may use formulas and computers to aid their work, they are still going to have to know when and how to use many mathematical principles to repair, update, and debug products and software and hardware.

> "If they like to tinker, they'd make good electrical or mechanical engineers."[4]
>
> —Craig Janus, electrical engineer

Get an Early Start

One thing is certain: If students are planning to apply to a college engineering program directly from high school, the earlier they start preparing for the field, the better. Many college engineering programs are highly competitive and accept only the top students from high schools around the country as well as internationally. High school students who know they are interested in pursuing an electrical engineering degree in college can benefit from taking classes such as algebra, trigonometry, calculus, biology, physics, chemistry, computer science, and word processing. Joining an extracurricular club that offers students an opportunity to participate in projects in which they build a computer, radio, drone, or robot can boost a student's chances of being accepted into a college engineering program. Working with a group of like-minded students on such a project can also give students a good sense of whether this type of work would be a good fit. Many other opportunities are also available in high school for those who want to try out engineering, including camps, competitions, and internships.

Opportunities to become more familiar with the engineering field are also available through professional organizations such as the Student Professional Awareness Committee, which works with student branches of the Institute of Electrical and Electronics Engineers (IEEE) in US universities. The organization provides career guidance and promotes student awareness of professional issues that impact electrical engineers. Through participation in Student Professional Awareness Conferences, one-day events that students organize and conduct, future electrical engineers hear practicing engineers discuss career issues such as professional ethics, licenses, and continuing education. The Student Professional Awareness Venture program offers students the opportunity to design their own career activities, with support from the Student Professional Awareness Committee. Some colleges and government organizations, such as the Massachusetts Institute of Technology (MIT) and the National Aeronautics and Space Administration (NASA), offer engineering competitions for high school students interested in electrical engineering.

The Next Step: Enroll in College

The next step in an electrical engineering career is to enter college. Even if a student did not find a passion for engineering in high school, it is not too late to pursue a two-year associate's degree to either catch up on the math and physics courses not

Using What You Learn

Electrical engineers often talk about how much they use what they learned in school. Edward Gonzales is an electromagnetic compatibility engineer at NASA's Jet Propulsion Laboratory in Pasadena, California. He says, "While some people like to say (almost proudly) that you never use what you learn in school, it has been the complete opposite in my case. . . . I've gone back to my class notes more times than I can count. It's refreshing to see that all those decades of school and tuition money get put to good use!"

Quoted in Andy Orin, "Career Spotlight: What I Do as a NASA Engineer," Lifehacker, July 28, 2015. https://lifehacker.com/.

taken during high school or to use it to apply to a four-year university. Community colleges, or junior colleges, typically offer a two-year degree in electrical engineering technology, which teaches students the basics of the field. Students focus on electrical theory and related principles and how these are used to test, alter, and debug electrical machinery and circuitry. Although a two-year degree will not be enough to land an electrical engineering job, it is enough to obtain a job as an electrical engineering tech, working under the guidance of an electrical engineer. According to Payscale.com, people with a two-year electrical engineering degree earn some of the highest salaries of those individuals with two-year degrees. An electrical engineering tech can work in a number of different settings, including commercial plants and laboratories. Since techs are trained at making calculations, running tests, and modifying equipment, they will find many opportunities that pay, on average, a salary in the mid-$40,000 range.

An Interdisciplinary Education

Promod Vohra, the academic dean of Northern Illinois University's College of Engineering and Engineering Technology, offers some advice to future electrical engineers about how to approach their education:

I would have liked my education to be more interdisciplinary. People need to have knowledge in other fields than their own. Engineers need to be able to solve problems in more than one field, and if they have the knowledge of those fields combined with the knowledge of engineering, they can provide solutions needed. . . . Take a lot of math and science classes, get a good score on the ACT [college admissions test] and pay attention to your class rank. I always say students should start taking their career seriously by the time they are in ninth grade.

Engineering Schools, "An Interview with Dean of Northern Illinois University's College of Engineering and Engineering Technology, Promod Vohra," Monster.com. http://engineeringschools.com.

A four-year college degree is required, however, for those individuals who wish to become an electrical engineer. Most career professionals suggest that a student choose a college engineering program that has been accredited by the Accreditation Board for Engineering and Technology, Inc. This group is a subgroup of the IEEE, the largest and most well-recognized of the professional organizations in the field. Employers often check to make sure that a student has graduated from such a program. It is also one of the prerequisites for obtaining a professional engineer license, which is required by some employers.

Most college students in engineering describe long days in the lab and lots of studying. Examinations are frequent and tough, and much of the work involves a lot of memorization. Because an electrical engineer may work in many different industries, engineering professors often recommend that students take classes in other engineering disciplines, such as chemical and biomedical engineering. In addition, most recommend that students take classes to hone their communication and writing skills. This is often a neglected topic when the career is discussed, but engineers rarely work alone; more often, they work on teams that include designers, techs, and other engineers. Therefore, they must be able to effectively communicate with everyone on the team. They must also write proposals and lead presentations in which they explain the technical aspects of their products to clients. Finally, they must document everything they work on so that another engineer can understand the specifications of the project as well as the reasoning behind the decisions that were made in the design and implementation of a product.

Internships

In addition to their academic workload, many engineering students decide to intern at a company while they go to school. Although internships are often voluntary or provide low pay, they can offer invaluable work experience and, occasionally, lead to a job at the company. Large corporations such as General Electric, Hewlett Packard, BAE Systems, and others typically hire one to three electrical engineering interns each year, but there are ample opportunities for internships outside of these large companies. Just a glance at available internships online shows a wide range of opportunities in a variety of industries, including an internship with a renewable energy company developing photovoltaic cells and an internship at the Mobile Corporation troubleshooting electrical circuitry.

Certification and Licensure

After obtaining an electrical engineering degree, some individuals seek one of two types of licensure. The first is the professional engineer (PE) license. In addition to their degree, PEs must have four years of work experience and pass a written exam called the Principles and Practice of Engineering.

Some students pursue another route to the same goal by taking and passing the Fundamentals of Engineering exam immediately after graduation. Those graduates are then designated as engineers in training or engineer interns. After acquiring work experience, they can take the final exam and gain a full PE certification. Some companies will not hire an engineer unless he or she has obtained this license.

CHAPTER 3

What Skills and Personal Qualities Matter Most— and Why?

Because an electrical engineer works in a technological environment that is always changing, a number of personality traits and skills are required to perform the job. Executives Ninh Tran and Xinwen Zhang of the employment website HireTeamMate give an overview of what they see as the most important qualities of an electrical engineer:

1. The best engineers have big-picture vision. They understand their product, architecture, and solution from the early moments of starting it to the end user experience and beyond. It's very critical for a successful engineer to possess a global view of what he or she is building and how it interacts with users, business clients, other technology, and the market. . . . For example, Mark Zuckerberg is a visionary engineer who builds his product from the ground with a strong vision of Facebook.

2. The best engineers are passionate. They are courageous and possess a can-do attitude. They are confident in their ability to figure out details and their ability to implement the most complex details into any project. Most successful engineers write clean and efficient code even when they take on projects requiring them to acquire a lot of knowledge, down to the most minute details. . . .

3. The best engineers are hands-on geeks with excellent execution skills. They think of something, and they

have the capability and drive to finish it. Engineering can be frustrating and also challenging at times, but the best engineers have developed a love for the process of innovation and have the ability to connect the dots and create solutions to overcome any obstacles to advance their product.[6]

A Critical Thinker with a Detail-Oriented Mind

As previously noted, an electrical engineer must possess many different abilities. Among the most important qualities are strong analytical and critical-thinking skills. Electrical engineers constantly face problems to solve, so they must be able to think at a very high level and analyze a problem in its entirety. Many engineers describe a desire to figure things out and understand how something works.

Another trait an electrical engineer must possess, which goes hand in hand with critical-thinking skills, is attention to detail.

"The best engineers are passionate."[6]

—Ninh Tran and Xinwen Zhang of the HireTeamMate employment website

Designs that electrical engineers work on are often intricate and involve many different components, including computer software and hardware that work together. Each line of code that is written and each solution that is attempted needs to be meticulously applied, as one simple error can mean a system does not work. Attention to detail is also necessary when debugging or running simulations to assess why a product or program is failing. Keeping meticulous records that detail where something is failing and which solutions have been tried is also part of an electrical engineer's job.

A Good Communicator

Many people are surprised to learn that electrical engineers must have excellent written and oral communication skills. Many outsiders, and even some prospective engineers, think the career attracts introverts. Yet engineers usually work as part of a team,

Analytical thinking and problem solving are essential qualities for electrical engineers. They must have a desire to understand how things work and the ability to figure things out.

with each member working on an aspect of a larger project. Therefore, each team member must be able to clearly communicate to the others what he or she is working on and how it fits into the overall picture. Engineers also often collaborate with others while working in review teams, on product launches, and during presentations for company management teams and clients. They may be required to translate complex technical solutions into easier-to-understand language so that others can get the gist of what they are working on. In addition, written skills are imperative. Electrical engineers must be able to write clearly and efficiently to document their projects. Many products that an engineer works on can be used for many years and will require technological updates. A clear history of the project and its updates will allow the next engineer who works on the product to come up to speed quickly to understand what may be required next.

William Leatherbury holds a master of science in electrical engineering and is a senior associate at the engineering firm Thornton Tomasetti. During his career, which has spanned more than forty years, he has hired many electrical engineers. Leatherbury says,

> Communication with other people and with both their peers and their superiors becomes an important part of their jobs, and many engineers are frightfully delinquent in these areas. So much of electrical engineering is regulated by adopted codes and leaves a lot of room for proper and good communications between the engineer and the installer. It is a rare engineer who can climb down from his warhorse and speak with the common worker. Few graduates can really communicate well in writing or speech.[7]

A Willingness to Learn New Things

Because the field of electrical engineering is highly technical, electrical engineers must be willing to constantly keep up with new technological developments in the field. This often means taking classes to learn new technologies and programs and reading a lot of research papers in electrical engineering publications. It all boils down to having a continuous curiosity and the discipline to be a lifelong learner. Nevin Altunyurt is an electromagnetic compatibility research engineer at the Ford Motor Company. In an interview with the EngineerGirl website, she highlights this need to constantly update one's knowledge:

> This is really important and it takes some effort, mostly a lot of reading. There are two parts to it. First, the industrial part requires keeping up with technological websites, trends, and blogs. At work we regularly receive these news digest emails that summarize hot topics, recent advancements and news in the automotive industry. I find these emails very useful to keep up with the industry. The second part

involves more technical details, learning new tools, reading academic papers, going to conferences and trainings to follow the latest research in my field. Because technology keeps on advancing, engineering requires constant learning. The technical landscape for electrical engineering changes continuously, and so one seeking this career must be continuously willing to learn new things, and stay up to date in developments in the field.[8]

The Qualities of a Good Engineer

Engineer Geoffrey Gaines works at the Lawrence Berkeley National Laboratory in Berkeley, California. In an online forum on November 22, 2014, he talked about the qualities he looks for when hiring an engineer:

> This depends somewhat on whether the applicant is entry level or senior, but for a senior EE [electrical engineer] I'd look for
>
> Accomplished—active in design, no dead wood
>
> Organized—every EE has a process, if the process is messy so is the design
>
> Humble—Arrogance begins when learning from one's mistakes ends. The majority of good EEs I've worked with have been humble
>
> Deliberate—the flip of a switch can do a lot of damage
>
> Reluctant to take shortcuts—in a complex design there are many temptations to cut corners
>
> Communicative—Willing and able to clearly argue for and teach their designs
>
> Open—willing to consider addition of features, a different communication interface, higher performance, greater safety factor, lower cost etc. Some fall in love with their work and are genuinely annoyed at the idea of changing it.

Quoted in Quora, "What Are Good Qualities to Look for When Interviewing an Electrical Engineer?," November 22, 2014. www.quora.com.

A Different Sort of Creativity

Although electrical engineers must have a deep understanding of mathematical and electronic fundamentals, they must also be creative in how they approach the job. David Butcher is a business editor and trade journalist. He argues that creativity is the most important aspect of the electrical engineer's job:

> Creativity is arguably the driving force behind innovation and therefore increasingly gaining recognition as the new capital in uncertain and challenging economic times. Innovation thrives on breakthrough thinking, nimbleness, and empowerment. Organizations often depend on big ideas and creative employees to develop innovative products and services. . . . In the engineering fields, creativity can be as valuable to solving a problem as the technical skills to identify and troubleshoot the source of the problem.[9]

This type of creativity, however, is different from that of an artist or other creative person. For the electrical engineer, creativity must also be rooted in logic. Watching a movie like *Back to the Future* with an electrical engineer, for example, would be no fun. The explanations of how a car can transmigrate space-time through an electrical short would likely cause the engineer to laugh in disbelief. The engineer uses his or her creativity within the scientific know-how of what is possible. Logical thinking is one of the important traits of the engineer. This logical thinking is often paired, however, with a dogged tenaciousness to attempt to make things work.

> "In the engineering fields, creativity can be as valuable to solving a problem as the technical skills to identify and troubleshoot the source of the problem."[9]
>
> —David Butcher, business editor and trade journalist

Steve Large is technology director for a UK company that makes and sells electric vehicle charging stations. He states, "You need to be tenacious. Sometimes people will tell you that what you want to do isn't possible, or that you 'can't do it like that.' You shouldn't let other people's opinions stop you. Engineers over the last 200 years have been looking for new ways of doing things with new materials and new pieces of technology."[10]

Because the field of electrical engineering is varied and serves as a cornerstone of so many industries, an electrical engineer must have many diverse traits to be successful. A detail-oriented and technological mind is required, and an ability to communicate with others, often in a team setting with individuals from many different perspectives, is also a requirement. A career in electrical engineering is deeply rooted in an understanding and acuity in mathematics and physics. It is a career in which experience is rewarded, yet a constant updating of oneself on the latest trends is a must.

CHAPTER 4

What Is It Like to Work as an Electrical Engineer?

A typical day for electrical engineers will vary depending on what industry they work in and what level of responsibility they have. Most, however, describe the typical day as a mix of sitting at a desk; working at a computer on a particular project; meeting with managers, fellow engineers, and technicians; and writing and reading. Many electrical engineers talk of the intellectual stimulation, the ability to work on many different projects, and the teamwork to be the highlights of their job. As Krista W. Murphy, an electrical engineer and the principal of Affiliated Engineers, explains, "No two days are ever the same. No two projects are ever the same. No two clients or coworkers are ever the same. There is always a challenge around the corner."[11]

Many Jobs, Many Industries

According to the Bureau of Labor Statistics (BLS), 324,600 electrical engineers worked in the United States in various specialties in 2016. Electrical engineers can master many specialties, and they usually do so during on-the-job training. Many remain at the same company for many years and gain a particular expertise based on their interests and skill sets.

Industries that employ electrical engineers are many and varied. Among them are mobile networking, banking, all branches of the military, power utility companies, international corporations that bring technologies to underdeveloped countries, transportation, Internet technology, biomedical fields, and pharmaceutical fields. According to the BLS, 14 percent of these engineers work for the federal government (excluding the postal service);

11 percent work for wired telecommunications carriers; 11 percent work in the semiconductor and other electronic component manufacturing arena; 8 percent work in architectural, engineering, and related services; and another 8 percent work in navigational, electromedical, and control instruments manufacturing. Electrical engineers work in a variety of other fields as well.

The Work Environment

In a typical day, an engineer can be seen studying technical manuals, articles, and other publications; designing, testing, and assembling devices; writing reports; and keeping track of various assignments. According to an article on the Princeton Review website, "Over 40 percent of the time is spent attending meetings, working on strategic planning, and tracking projects."[12] Although all electrical engineers spend time in the office working at a computer, some are outdoors in the field for part of the day. Others travel internationally helping to install and troubleshoot programs that their company sells overseas.

> "Over 40 percent of the time is spent attending meetings, working on strategic planning, and tracking projects."[12]
>
> —Princeton Review

Many electrical engineering projects take a long time and require many changes before they are released to a client. The average span of time from the initial design of a project to its actual release is two years. Therefore, patience and tenacity are essential in the profession. Rick Fulton, a lifelong electrical engineer in weapon systems, adds that "thoroughness" is also required. He says, "It's more than just being detail-oriented. It's anticipating what can and will go wrong and putting a product through many different tests to make sure it will run in the field."[13]

Daily Communication

Many electrical engineers say that communication makes up a large part of their workday. For example, at Walt Disney Imagineering in Florida, where they help design rides and attractions, a typical workday might see an electrical engineer joining colleagues

What Is Your Day Like?

The staff of the career website OwlGuru.com conducted a survey of electrical engineers that asked about their typical workday. The following are some of the questions and answers:

Do you have telephone conversations
every day in this job? • • • • • • • • • • • 62 percent said yes

Do you have to use email every day
in this job? • • • • • • • • • • • • • • • • • 98 percent said yes

How important is it to work in a team
in this job? • • • • • • • • • • • • • • • • 64 percent said very important

Do you have group discussions every
day in this job? • • • • • • • • • • • • • • 72 percent said yes

Do you have to meet strict deadlines
every day in this job? • • • • • • • • • • • 18 percent said yes

Do you talk or work with customers
every day in this job? • • • • • • • • • • • 23 percent said yes

Do you have to deal with angry
customers every day in this job? • • • • • 0 percent said yes

Do you have to make decisions every
day in this job? • • • • • • • • • • • • • • 27 percent said yes

OwlGuru.com, "What Do Electrical Engineers Do: Job Description, Responsibilities and Duties."
www.owlguru.com.

in trying to understand what circuitry, power systems, and other electrical gadgetry are required to power a ride. Electrical engineer Jody Gerstner is a technical director of control systems for Walt Disney Imagineering. Among his many duties, Gerstner manages other engineers. He believes the most important part of his daily work is communication:

I'm acting as the engineers' agent to make sure that they have everything they need to get their projects completed. . . . An outgoing personality is mandatory, in my opinion, if you want to grow in this job because you have to communicate. . . . You have to bridge the gap between pure technical stuff and hands on, how to put it together. So, if you can't communicate, then no one will know what you have to offer, and no one will know how to build what you are conceptualizing.[14]

Those electrical engineers who are good at communicating usually rise to management positions. Sangeeta Kodukula holds an electrical engineering degree and is a systems engineer for Cisco Systems in Texas. She heads a team of sales engineers who work on cybersecurity technology. She explains, "For my work I do a lot of presenting, public speaking, as well as study technology! I like that my work is a mix of both business and technical aptitude."[15]

Opportunities in Renewable Resources

Newer industries, such as renewable resource companies, hire electrical engineers to design products, aid in the development of installation plans, and troubleshoot problems as they occur. For example, electrical engineers are being hired to help develop wind farms. In this capacity, electrical engineers scout the appropriate site to see how to bring power to the location. They also design the turbines and figure out how many are needed and where they should be situated. In addition, they determine how the energy generated at the wind farm will be sent to the power grid.

In a job such as this one, engineers are required to know the conditions of the site where the wind farm will be located. Thus, the electrical engineers must visit the site to see where the turbines will be laid out, if there are any land obstacles that will be tricky to navigate, and how the overall design will work to bring the energy generated by the turbines to a collection site. Back at the office, the engineers use software programs to calculate how much energy each turbine can be expected to produce and

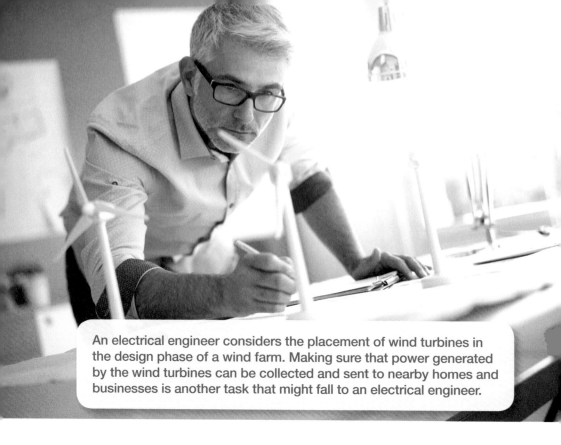

An electrical engineer considers the placement of wind turbines in the design phase of a wind farm. Making sure that power generated by the wind turbines can be collected and sent to nearby homes and businesses is another task that might fall to an electrical engineer.

to determine the overall budget of the project. Part of the day is spent reporting these findings during meetings with managers and other engineers on the team. They may be asked to redo particular aspects of the design or make suggestions to accommodate changes.

Hours and Locations May Vary

Most electrical engineers work full-time. Although the job does not typically require overtime, it may be required for several weeks or months to complete a particular job. Some engineers work for companies that have a multistate or international presence, and they may be asked to travel to those locations for weeks at a time. Rick Fulton spent six months away from his family in California to work in Phoenix, Arizona, to help install a system for his company, BAE Systems. "The pay was great, and that's why I did it, but my marriage and family life suffered. Of the six engineers that decided to take that job, four were divorced within the next three years. They all attributed it to the time they spent away from home."[16]

Engineer Matt Reeves works for a renewable energy start-up company and must travel to Europe several times a year. He leaves his wife and young son for two weeks at a time. While his wife, Heidi, says it can be hard, she knows it is part of the job. When their son is a bit older, she hopes to be able to travel with Matt and sightsee while he is at work.

Some engineers take the traveling part to an even greater extreme. They work for companies that install electrical projects in underdeveloped countries. In such cases, engineers may be gone for months at a time. For the most part, engineers who leave the country to pursue these jobs are usually at the start of their careers, before they have a lot of other life commitments.

Salaries

Salaries for electrical engineers are on a par with many other engineering occupations. According to the BLS, starting salaries averaged $59,133 in 2016. The average salary for an electrical engineer is $88,530, and top salaries are around $130,120. To earn a higher salary, most electrical engineers obtain an advanced degree, usually a master's degree or a doctorate, in a specialty. Some specialties include communications and signal processing, computer engineering, controls, electrophysics, microelectronics, and power systems. Kathlene West, who holds a bachelor's degree in electrical engineering and a master's in power management, works as a power engineer for Dayton Power and Light Company in Ohio. She recommends that electrical engineers gain a specialty:

> "Become an expert on something."[17]
>
> —Kathlene West, electrical engineer

Become an expert on something. Sometimes young engineers are fast-tracked from one position to the next. This can be great for your career but may leave you without an area of mastery. It's prudent to have some depth in one or more technical areas. Job security is never guaranteed and your technical expertise might make all the difference if you need to re-establish your career after a layoff or relocation.[17]

Advancement and Other Job Opportunities

Electrical engineering is one of the most versatile of the engineering disciplines. And because electrical power is essential to technology, electrical engineers are uniquely positioned to play a vital role in developing the ideas of the future. As technology advances and new electrical engineering specialties emerge, careers in this profession will continue to be in demand. With a bachelor's degree in electrical engineering and a license with the IEEE, electrical engineers start their careers with a great base salary and a wealth of job opportunities. As they work hard and gain experience in a particular field, they can also advance in their careers. Likewise, engineers who earn advanced degrees, usually a master's degree or a doctorate in a particular specialty, have even more job prospects.

Firmware and Computer Engineering

Electrical engineers often move easily into computer engineering and firmware design, maintenance, and debugging because of their expertise in programming languages and computer hardware, and an understanding of the interaction between the two. Both electrical and computer engineering require knowledge of many of the same subjects. The courses for the two disciplines overlap—they both need to understand power systems and energy conversion, semiconducting devices and circuits, and electromagnetic fields and waves. However, electrical engineer Thomas Crosley argues that an electrical engineering degree is even more versatile than a software engineering degree:

With a EE [electrical engineering] degree, but with an interest in software, you would be an ideal candidate for a job in firmware development. . . . With a EE degree, you would also be qualified to design the hardware itself if that interested you. As a firmware engineer for nearly four decades (I started in the mid 70's), I have found it is easier for an EE to learn programming skills than a CS [computer science] major [to] learn EE skills.[18]

> "I have found it is easier for an EE [electrical engineer] to learn programming skills than a CS [computer science] major learn EE skills."[18]
>
> —Thomas Crosley, electrical engineer

Many electrical engineers interested in firmware or software engineering pursue an additional degree in computer engineering. Just glancing through online job listings proves that many employers in this industry are willing to hire math, physics, and engineering majors, too. According to the website Best Computer Science Degrees, which ranks degree programs,

> In general, you should be able to get a computer science job with an electrical engineering degree, because engineering programs usually require quite a few math classes. Employers tend to look for applicants with math abilities because people who are good at math are usually good at solving problems, and all computer science jobs require people with problem-solving skills. It's fairly easy to teach employees about specific programming languages, but it's a lot harder to teach them how to solve problems.[19]

According to the BLS, this specialty earns about $96,000 a year, though one can earn as much as $129,000.

Controls Engineer

Another career that an electrical engineering graduate can pursue is controls engineer. These engineers are the so-called big-picture engineers who analyze and design electrical systems. They are

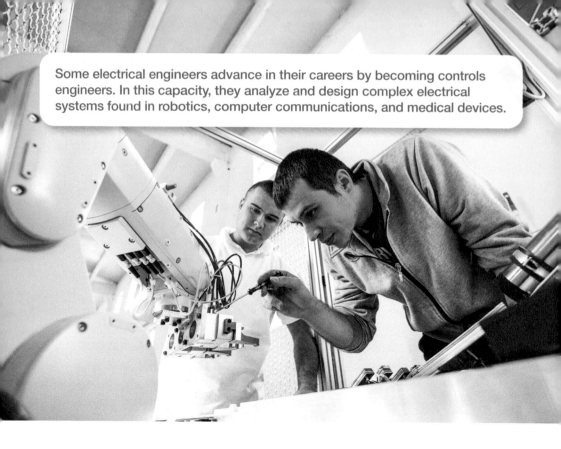

Some electrical engineers advance in their careers by becoming controls engineers. In this capacity, they analyze and design complex electrical systems found in robotics, computer communications, and medical devices.

often the electrical engineers who manage complex projects that involve technicians from many different areas. As such, they not only have to have strong technical backgrounds but also must be great communicators and team leaders. Some of the products these engineers might work on include automobile antilock braking systems, robotic manufacturing assembly lines, computer communications systems, spaceflight control systems, and cardiac pacemakers. They work in concert with chemical, mechanical, and computer engineers to integrate and coordinate the many different components of the product or system. According to Salary.com, as of early 2018 the average salary of a controls engineer was $68,317, with a range between $61,367 and $72,825.

Project Engineer

Like controls engineers, electrical engineers who become project engineers coordinate projects with many people from different technical backgrounds, usually within a corporation or a municipal agency. However, the project engineer's responsibilities are larger in scope and typically require more reporting to the managers in the organization. They must keep the projects within budget and on schedule for completion, and they must foster communication between everyone involved in the project.

Many job opportunities across industries are available for project engineers. A job posting from the Occidental Petroleum Corporation, an international oil and gas exploration and production company, lists some of the primary duties of a project engineer:

> Development and execution of projects for . . . electrical distribution and transmission system; including the management of engineering and design, standards, and daily project management from purchase power locations through end use points. Also provides new electrical technology solutions that encompass the entire [Occidental] organization to help make the electrical teams more effective and efficient while also providing benefits to other teams within the organization.[20]

Some of the job's other duties include meeting with managers, working with others on staff to achieve project goals, providing customer support, and managing the electrical tools and equipment used by those on the team. The average salary in 2016 for an electrical project engineer was $103,486, according to the BLS.

Electrical Design Engineer

Another career choice for those with a degree in electrical engineering is an electrical design engineer. The simplest explanation of this career is that it involves the design of electrical systems, including lighting systems, power distribution systems, electronic components, and voice and data communications. Because these systems can be in a variety of industries, electrical design engineers can work in robotics, electrical substations, or in computer and digital circuit design, to name a few.

On the employment search engine Indeed, a job listing for an electrical design engineer at Isolite Systems, a medical technology company specializing in dentistry, gives a good example of the qualities required for this job:

> You will be responsible for the complete design and development of Class I and Class II electro-mechanical medical products. Requires coordination of both internal and external resources, to achieve goals in a timely manner, cost effectively and in alignment with market needs, cost constraints and regulatory requirements. Must have experience in communication, lighting, power conversion & distribution, designing circuits and electronic assemblies, writing and debugging software/firmware, general formal engineering documentation, hands-on testing and troubleshooting, and engineering oversight for manufacturing, assembly, and installation of equipment.[21]

The ad also emphasizes that the candidate needs strong analytical and problem-solving skills and must have excellent written, oral, and presentation skills. This job is just one example of how electrical engineers, as they take on more responsibility, must also have strong managerial and communication skills to succeed. The BLS cites the average salary in 2016 for this specialty as $128,222. Again, these jobs are available in any industry.

Systems Engineer

Another career in which individuals can use their degree in electrical engineering is systems engineer. This specialty can be found in both the corporate and civil fields. Engineers in these jobs usually are responsible for computer systems, servers, and other electrical hardware. This is one of the most technical jobs for an electrical engineer, and although jobs are available for the entry-level engineer, most jobs in this field require several years of on-the-job experience. In fact, a systems engineer is one of the most highly paid careers. The BLS cited the average salary in 2016 as $141,894.

One job advertisement on Indeed seeks a systems engineer for an automotive engineering company that designs electrical

Salaries Differ Depending on Where You Live

The salary of an electrical engineer is influenced by where in the country he or she lives. Electrical engineers earn more on the West Coast, for example. The yearly average salary in this area is $98,642—and that is across all specialties in the field. In New York and the northeastern portion of the country, the average salary is $88,118. The Southeast and Midwest trail behind, with median salaries of $82,814 and $79,429.

systems, including connectors, wiring assemblies and harnesses, electrical centers, and hybrid high voltage and safety distribution systems. The job also requires electrical work on infotainment and displays; 3D clusters, embedded WiFi, navigation, and other components. The job requires a strong electrical hardware background with working knowledge of systems engineering tools. The candidate is also required to understand embedded control software and software development.

Machine Learning

A relatively new career field for an electrical engineering graduate is that of machine learning. This field combines electrical engineering with computer science; therefore, employers often require applicants to have a master's degree in computer science. Machine learning is a field in which computers are given the ability to learn a task without being specifically programmed to do so. Computers use algorithms and data that they compute in real time to learn to negotiate a task. Machine learning is being used in self-driving car technology, for example.

Electrical engineer George Sung turned his bachelor's degree in computer engineering and his master's in electrical engineering into a career working in the field of machine learning. To educate himself about machine learning, Sung took advantage of several open online courses in web development, Android development, machine learning, and artificial intelligence. He also took classes in self-driving car technology through the online university Udacity. Sung ended up as a machine learning engineer with the automotive company BMW, working with a team to develop a self-driving car. Sung pursued his dream of a career in this new discipline by having the tenacity and desire to seek it out without an organized program to follow. With a background in electrical engineering first, however, he was able to enter this nascent field.

> "Great engineers possess a technology vision for the next decade. They follow closely new technology trends and try to keep current with the latest innovations."[22]
>
> —John Vespasian, the author of many self-help career books

The flexibility to work in such a wide variety of specialties may be one of the best reasons to pursue an electrical engineering degree. For those students who enjoy new technologies and the opportunity to learn new tasks and acquire new knowledge, the degree can be used to enter many new fields. Author John Vespasian talks about this quality of pursuing the next trend as an essential part of the electrical engineer's career path:

This is the character trait that separates truly remarkable engineers from the rest. Great engineers possess a technology vision for the next decade. They follow closely new technology trends and try to keep current with the latest innovations. They have a clear idea of the additional skills they want to acquire in the next ten years, and they foresee which trends are going to dominate the technology markets in the next years. Such a vision is something that engineers can only develop if they are deeply interested in their field and in new technology applications.[22]

CHAPTER 6

What Does the Future Hold for Electrical Engineers?

According to the BLS, the future looks stable for electrical engineers. Overall employment of electrical and electronics engineers is projected to grow by 7 percent through 2026, about as fast as the average for all occupations. This growth will occur even though the rate of growth for manufacturing industries that hire electrical and electronics engineers is expected to slow or decline.

The BLS also predicts that job growth in the field will largely be in the area of consumer electronics as demand for better and more sophisticated technology continues to grow. This demand is expected to fuel careers for electrical engineers in research and development, as well as design. Continued interest in environmental technologies will fuel developments in solar and hybrid technologies. Advancements in communications and semiconductors will also contribute to the demand for electrical engineers. The nation's need for an upgrade to its power grids will also ensure plenty of jobs for future electrical engineers.

Electrical engineers themselves agree that these new technologies will create future jobs. Arieta M.L. Gonelevu, the senior project officer for the International Union for Conservation of Nature, believes that electrical engineering jobs will be plentiful as new technologies are developed:

> Jobs for engineers in the future will be more innovative and challenging as lots of technologies have been piloted now and will be commercially available in the future. Students

"Jobs for engineers in the future will be more innovative and challenging as lots of technologies have been piloted now and will be commercially available in the future."[23]

—Arieta M.L. Gonelevu, the senior project officer for the International Union for Conservation of Nature

should take time to read and research on these technologies whilst at university and not to totally rely on theory/what the lecturers have designed for the course. Students who undertake research should choose topics that can be further utilized when they go out into the working world. . . . The move is towards sustainable development and addressing environmental issues, so one should be well versed with that too.[23]

Opportunities to Upgrade the Infrastructure

Some engineers point out that as the infrastructure of the United States evolves, there will be a need to upgrade and retool many of the existing systems. Integrating these systems with new technologies will keep demand high for electrical engineers. Engineer Kathlene West emphasizes the importance of learning about power systems:

> The power and energy industry is undergoing a lot of change right now. Distributed generation, increasing use of renewables such as wind and solar, distribution automation, and a constantly shifting regulatory environment are just a few examples. Although I can't predict exactly how this industry will take shape in the years to come, it's safe to say that complexity will increase. That means more work for protection and control engineers. Students looking to enter this field might want to consider schools offering power systems as an area of emphasis.[24]

Others point to the fact that as the largest generation of US citizens reaches retirement age, many jobs will be opening up, especially at a time when young engineers are being trained in

Electrical engineers will be essential in future efforts to manage growing energy needs for people around the world. In many cities, states, and countries efforts are already under way to develop and use smart grids, but there is still much work to be done.

new technologies. In an online interview, Cheri Warren, assistant to the chief executive officer of National Grid, a company that provides utilities in New York, Rhode Island, and Massachusetts, describes the current and future need for electrical engineers:

The power industry has and will continue to have a huge need for engineers. With the tri-challenge of climate, security of energy supplies and affordability, there is more than enough work to go around. We are now designing smarter grids, replacing power systems that were built by Edison and Westinghouse, and changing the way people interact with energy. Nearly 50% of our work force will retire . . . [soon]. That creates huge opportunity for engineers and a promise of exciting careers![25]

High-Tech Opportunities

Along with these more traditional engineering roles, plenty of opportunity exists for those electrical engineers who want to work on the most advanced technologies. These include medical device technology and circuitry that use ultrasmall, embedded chips called ULSI (short for ultra-large-scale integration). This new technology can place more than 1 million circuit elements on a single chip. Some electrical engineers working with this breakthrough technology view the future as an exciting place. Just as the computer changed the way most of us live today, these ever-smaller and highly connected chips will change electrical engineering. More and more information can be placed on the chips. So devices will become smaller and will be able to do more complex tasks. In addition, advances in artificial intelligence and machine learning will fuel new careers for electrical engineers who specialize in microtechnology.

"Nearly 50% of our work force will retire . . . [soon]. That creates huge opportunity for engineers and a promise of exciting careers!"[25]

—Cheri Warren, the assistant to the chief executive officer of National Grid

The history of electric lighting is a good example of how electrical engineers made changes to products to keep up with technology. Although electricity generation is split between commercial, industrial, and residential uses, 19 percent of electricity is still used for lighting. To force manufacturers to come up with more energy-efficient lighting, the Energy Independence and Security Act was passed in 2007. The act required manufacturers to phase out the production and sale of incandescent lights. Although the measure was defunded, electrical engineers were busily finding replacements for incandescent lighting. They designed LED lighting as a replacement. LED technology is so cheap and available that

Career of the Future

Students interested in futuristic careers will likely not be disappointed by pursuing a degree in electrical engineering. In this excerpt, Nader Mowlaee, an electronics engineer who works as an engineering career coach and technical recruiter, shares why he thinks that the car industry will need electrical engineers.

"I grew up in a family of mechanics, I have always been a crazy car guy and a real automotive enthusiast a.k.a. Petrol Head. Quite naturally I have always been attracted to working with automotive firms, helping them hire top-level electrical engineers, controls, and system programmers."

However, now that the world's leading automotive manufacturers are focusing on developing fully electric and autonomous vehicles, they have become desperate to find electrical engineers who are adept at designing and developing such systems.

Nader Mowlaee, "Top 3 Industries for Highest Electrical Engineer Salary," *Interesting Engineering*, November 1, 2016. https://interestingengineering.com.

many consumers now choose this lighting source over incandescent lighting, even though there are no laws that prevent the latter's use.

For electrical engineers who want to pursue the research and development side of the profession, the future will be filled with technologies that resemble the stuff of science fiction movies today. Microtechnology, for example, will eventually permeate people's lives in new and interesting ways. Electrical engineering researchers and others interested in microtechnology are currently studying the ways that LEDs gather heat from the environment. With that knowledge, they might be able to develop microchips that convert body heat into energy. These chips could then replace batteries in various devices. Some of the more interesting theories in this area include a microcardiogram, a device the size of a Band-Aid that monitors a patient's heart rate. Engineers are also developing eyeglasses that contain an embedded chip. If the eyeglasses are wirelessly connected to a smartphone with voice-recognition software, they would allow a hearing-impaired person wearing such lenses to see the speaker's words translated into captions.

The Internet of Things

Indeed, some electrical engineers see a day when everything will be connected to a wireless interface. Called the Internet of Things (IoT), the idea is that everything, even a key fob or pen, could connect to the Internet. Embedded software engineer Ken Davidson explains that electrical engineers will be behind the development of such devices in the future:

> Twenty-five years ago, while developing the Circuit Cellar Home Control System (HCS) II, our group created a series of interface boards that could be placed around the house and communicate [using a common interface]. Tons of discrete wire running throughout buildings was the norm at the time, and the idea of running just a single twisted pair between units was novel and exciting. This all predated inexpensive Ethernet and public Internet. Today, such distributed intelligence has only gotten better, smaller, and cheaper. With the Internet of Things (IoT) everybody is talking about, it's not unusual to find a wireless interface and embedded intelligence right down to the level of a light bulb. There was an episode of *The Big Bang Theory* where the guys set up the apartment lights so they could be controlled from anywhere in the world. Everyone got a laugh when the "geeks" were excited when someone from Japan was blinking their lights. But the idea of such embedded intelligence and remote access continuing to evolve and improve truly is exciting. I look forward to the day in the not-too-distant future when such control is commonplace to most people and not just a geeky novelty.[26]

So, whether students want to work on upgrading existing technologies or move into the most cutting-edge fields of the future, electrical engineering might be the degree for them. Many engineers in the field see a bright future for electrical engineers. This versatile degree can lead to a long-lasting career in electrical engineering, be combined with advanced degrees, or remain a foundational degree for many other opportunities.

Interview with an Electrical Engineer

Jose Berroteran is an electrical engineer at BAE Systems in San Diego, California. BAE is a British multinational defense, security, and aerospace company. Berroteran has been working as an electrical engineer for six years and is in the process of obtaining a higher degree. He discussed his career during an interview with the author.

Q: Why did you become an electrical engineer?

A: I was always good at math and science courses, and I enjoy solving problems. I am originally from Venezuela, and in that country, we have a different way of looking at what type of careers are acceptable. If you are going to choose a career that you plan on advancing in throughout your life, you have to become something like a doctor, lawyer, or engineer. I chose electrical engineering in particular because I have a couple of uncles who are also engineers. I knew that if I ever have to return to Venezuela for family reasons, I would definitely be able to get a job with them.

Q: Can you describe your typical workday?

A: Most of my workday is solving problems. In my job much of the work is to redesign something, usually a circuit board, that has already been designed once, but because of changes in the final product, it requires a redesign. I am also required to document any changes that I make to the existing design. I also work with other engineers on my team, who test my work and help me to solve problems I may be having.

Q: What do you like most about your job?

A: I like working alongside people with tons of experience. I am one of the youngest engineers on my team. These engineers have helped me a lot to learn new ways of approaching problems. For example, in debugging products, they have shown me ways to streamline the process and target what is causing a problem quicker. It is the difference between learning on the job, with time constraints and with real problems, rather than in school, where there are fewer restrictions on time.

Q: What do you like least about your job?

A: The way large corporations make decisions. For example, it can sometimes take a very long time to make a very simple decision because many people have to be involved in the process.

Q: What personal qualities do you find most valuable for this type of engineering work?

A: Though there are many important qualities, one is an ability to communicate your ideas and thoughts to your peers. Since all work involves being on a team, and all projects involve multiple people, it is extremely important to be able to communicate to all of those people. Although this quality is most important for people who want to go into management, I want to remain an engineer, and there are other ways other than speech to communicate. For example, I can show my teammates my work, my solution, and they can test it empirically to see if it works. You can even check documentation, schematics, and firmware.

In school, for example, professors and students are from all over the world, and for many English is a second language, not their first. Yet we can all communicate because we are working on something that involves objective mathematical and scientific knowledge, not language skills.

For this reason I think being able to think logically is extremely important. Being able to follow the parameters of a project, know how to use science and math to lead you to a solution the fastest way possible is most important.

Q: Why are you pursuing a higher degree?

A: I am going for my master of science in electrical engineering. The main reason is to broaden my job options in case I need to move to be closer to my family who are living in Los Angeles. The second reason is to maximize my earning potential. Based on my online research and interviewing other engineers, they all agree that pursuing a higher degree will lead to better earnings.

I am going to school to specialize in VLSI systems at San Diego State University. [Editor's Note: VLSI, or very large-scale integration, is the process of creating computer microchips that contain hundreds of thousands of transistors.] This specialty is the closest thing to what I already do at my current job. I hope that it will help supply me with more practical information to help solve the real-world problems I am encountering on the job. I am also taking more courses in radio frequency and digital signal processing.

I like microprocessors because it is still working with hardware, something you can see and feel. Much of electrical engineering is about software, which is always changing and cannot be seen.

Q: What is the best way to prepare for this type of engineering job?

A: I think the best way to prepare for any engineering job is to have hands-on skills. It helps to have done useful projects in school or on your own.

Q: What other advice do you have for students who might be interested in a career as an electrical engineer?

A: If you are truly interested in becoming an engineer, take online courses. You can gain valuable and applicable knowledge and be a better job prospect than somebody with just a degree. All you need is to be willing to learn.

Electrical engineering is a tough major. You really have no time for anything other than school. The classes are tough, the labs are tough, and you are always working as hard as you can. So you really have to like to work hard and be immersed in school.

SOURCE NOTES

Chapter 1: What Does an Electrical Engineer Do?

1. Tesla, "Senior Electrical Engineer: Power Electronics," Glassdoor, job posting. www.glassdoor.com.

2. Ira A. Fulton College of Engineering and Technology, Electrical and Computer Engineering, "Electrical vs. Computer Engineering," Brigham Young University. https://ece.byu.edu.

Chapter 2: How Do You Become an Electrical Engineer?

3. Quoted in TryEngineering.org, "Life of an Engineer: Aravinda Paranagama." http://tryengineering.org.

4. Quoted in Cathy Sivak, "An Interview with Craig Janus, Electrical Engineer," EngineeringSchools.com. http://engineeringschools.com.

5. WeUseMath.org, "Electrical Engineer." http://weusemath.org.

Chapter 3: What Skills and Personal Qualities Matter Most—and Why?

6. Quoted in Angela Stringfellow, "20 Engineering Professionals Reveal the Most Important Traits of Successful Electrical Engineers," *Pannam Blog*, Pannam Imaging, March 3, 2017. www.pannam.com.

7. Quoted in Quora, "What Are Good Qualities to Look for When Interviewing an Electrical Engineer?," October 28, 2014. www.quora.com.

8. Quoted in Grace Lam, "Interview with Nevin Altunyurt," EngineerGirl, August 11, 2015. www.engineergirl.org.

9. Quoted in Stringfellow, "20 Engineering Professionals Reveal the Most Important Traits of Successful Electrical Engineers."

10. Quoted in Stringfellow, "20 Engineering Professionals Reveal the Most Important Traits of Successful Electrical Engineers."

Chapter 4: What Is It Like to Work as an Electrical Engineer?

11. Quoted in EngineerGirl, "I'm an Engineer: Ms. Krista W. Murphy." www.engineergirl.org.

12. Princeton Review, "A Day in the Life of an Electrical Engineer." www.princetonreview.com.

13. Rick Fulton, interview with the author, January 15, 2018.

14. Quoted in TryEngineering.org, "Life of an Engineer: Jody Gerstner." http://tryengineering.org.

15. Quoted in EngineerGirl, "I'm an Engineer: Sangeeta Kodukula." www.engineergirl.org.

16. Fulton, interview.

17. Quoted in TryEngineering.org, "Life of an Engineer: Kathlene West, P.E." http://tryengineering.org.

Chapter 5: Advancement and Other Job Opportunities

18. Quoted in Workplace Stack Exchange, "Can I Get a Software Development Job with an EE Degree?," May 9, 2013. https://workplace.stackexchange.com.

19. Best Computer Science Degrees, "Can You Get a Computer Science Job with an Electrical Engineering Degree?" www.bestcomputersciencedegrees.com.

20. Occidental Petroleum Corporation, project manager job listing. https://oxy.taleo.net.

21. Isolite Systems, "Staff Electrical Design Engineer," Indeed. www.indeed.com.

22. Quoted in Stringfellow, "20 Engineering Professionals Reveal the Most Important Traits of Successful Electrical Engineers."

Chapter 6: What Does the Future Hold for Electrical Engineers?

23. Quoted in TryEngineering.org, "Life of an Engineer: Arieta M.L. Gonelevu." http://tryengineering.org.

24. Quoted in TryEngineering.org, "Life of an Engineer: Kathlene West, P.E."

25. Quoted in TryEngineering.org, "Life of an Engineer: Cheri Warren." http://tryengineering.org.

26. Quoted in Circuit Cellar, "Seven Engineers on the Future of Electrical Engineering," December 30, 2014. http://circuitcellar.com.

FIND OUT MORE

American Society for Engineering Education (ASEE)

1818 N St. NW, Suite 600
Washington, DC 20036
www.asee.org

The ASEE develops policies and programs that enhance professional opportunities for engineering faculty members. It also promotes activities that support increased student enrollments in engineering and engineering technology at colleges and universities.

Institute of Electrical and Electronics Engineers-USA (IEEE-USA)

2001 L St. NW
Washington, DC 20036
www.ieeeusa.org

The IEEE-USA informs and educates IEEE members in the United States about trends, issues, and actions affecting their professional careers. The group prepares positions and recommends appropriate action to public and private decision makers and responds to member requests for information.

International Electrotechnical Commission (IEC)

Regional Centre for North America
446 Main St., Sixteenth Floor
Worcester, MA 01608
www.iec.ch

The IEC is the world's leading organization for the preparation and publication of international standards for all electrical, electronic, and related technologies, known collectively as electrotechnology. The IEC offers a series of lectures and provides access to a selection of working documents for academic institutions worldwide.

Technology Student Association (TSA)
1914 Association Dr.
Reston, VA 20191
www.tsaweb.org

The TSA fosters personal growth, leadership, and opportunities in technology, innovation, design, and engineering. Members integrate science, technology, engineering, and mathematics concepts through cocurricular activities, competitive events, and related programs.

INDEX

PICTURE CREDITS

cover: zoranm/iStockphoto.com

 6: Maury Aaseng

10: Petrovich9/iStockphoto.com

25: skynesher/iStockphoto.com

34: goodluz/Shutterstock.com

38: Drazen_/Shutterstock.com

45: ablokhin/iStockphoto.com

Bonnie Szumski has written many nonfiction books for young adults during her thirty-plus-year career.